for a very special friend
with love

The Gift of Friendship

A Verse of Love
For My Best Friend

FRIENDS GIFT SERIES

All images and illustrations included in this book are in the public domain.
Text is written by Violet Jade.

Family is essential for survival. Friends are essential for surviving our family.

— *Thadeus Blackwell*

Note from the author

If you are lucky enough to be a recipient of this book, a congratulations are in order. This means that you have a friend who undoubtedly cares deeply about you, and that is not something that should ever be taken for granted. Over the last few years, study after study has shown that loneliness does far more than affect our quality of life; it can also be detrimental to our physical health and wellbeing. This is particularly troubling as we as a society continue to build walls between us and other humans, choosing instead to interact with technological devices, most of which were, ironically, intended to help us connect with other humans. It's crucial that we reverse this trend, and hopefully, this book will play a small part in deepening your bond with the lovely person who gifted you this book. It is my sincere hope that the words in this book reflect the deepness of your friendship, and that this very special relationship will endure and deepen for many years to come.

Enjoy!

— *Violet Jade*

In our lives we have our crew, a group of friends to help us through ...

The crew is great, but soon we knew there's something special between me and you.

For reasons I still can't comprehend, the two of us became best friends.

We talked and talked,
it never grew old.
No topic off limits,
no joke untold.

And with this gift, what I aim to do ...

Is to express the ways I appreciate you.

Like how you comfort when I'm feeling blue ...

And how you find fun things to do.

With you,
all is better,
even when life
is mundane ...

Like the time we got stuck out in the rain.

Or the time when you let me share your drink ...

And when I was too sad to speak.

Or that time you reminded me to bring a sweater ...

Or the time you told me that I deserved better.

Or the times we needed to have a brutal conversation ...

Or the times we dressed all wrong for the occasion.

And even when what happened was what we'd feared ...

And when that party just got weird.

And looking back at how we used to dress ...

And at all the ease, and all the stress ...

For you, I have but one request:

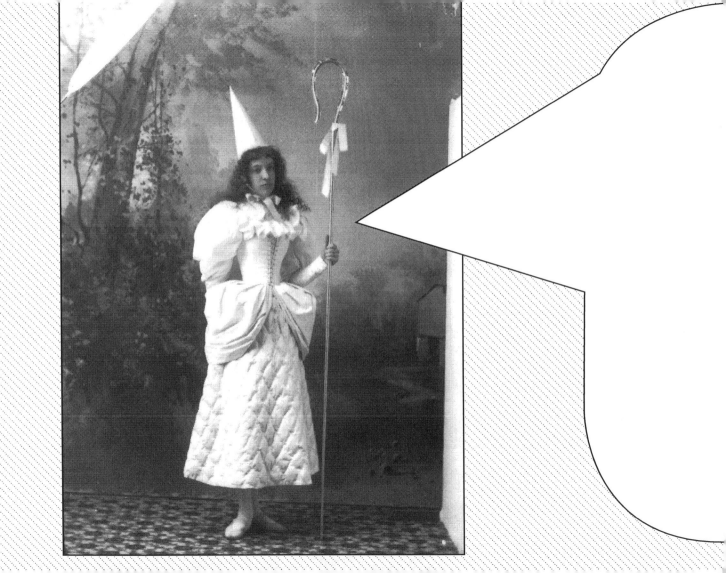

Tell me, how do I look in this dress?

You're the only one I can ask without fear ...

Who will tell me what I need to hear.

Besides, along this life's scenic route ...

It's obvious that we look cute.

Sure, we butt heads every now and then ...

But I never wonder whose corner you're in.

And no one will come between us two ...

AND I PITY THE PERSON WHO SAYS MEAN THINGS ABOUT YOU!

When
I need
help ...

I don't have to ask,

Even when it's an unpleasant task.

You help me

keep my life

on track ...

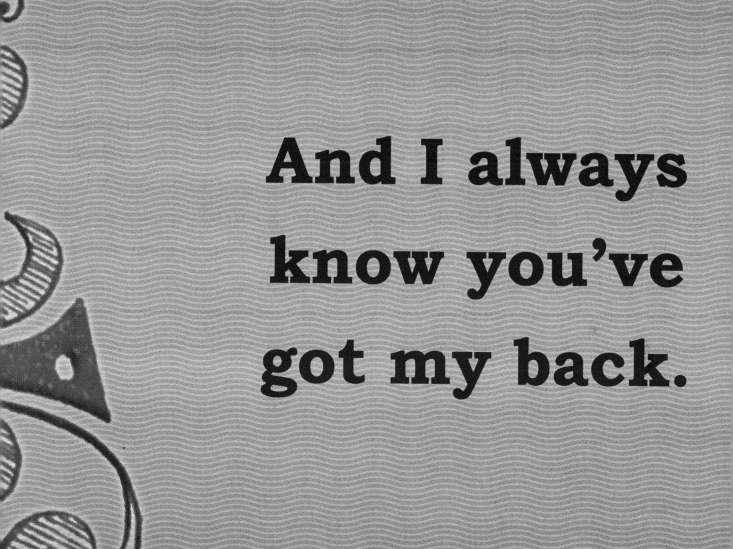

And I always know you've got my back.

You always know just how to respond ...

And no one else quite "gets" our bond.

And as you read through this string of rhymes ...

Think back upon those lovely times ...

There's been
dancing ...

And dancing ...

And dancing …

And there's

more to do,

And I don't know what I'd do without you.

And when I think about what we've been through ...

It reminds me how much ...

I love you!

And I know that our good times are far from done ...

More memories to make for years to come.

We hope you've enjoyed your copy of The Gift of Friendship. Hopefully this book has helped express feelings of love between you and a very special person in your life.

GOOD GIFT Books

If you enjoyed this book, you might also like The Gift of Sisterhood.

The Gift of Sisterhood

A TRIBUTE TO THE BEST SISTER IN THE WORLD

51403425R00057

Made in the USA
Lexington, KY
03 September 2019